T0143737

# PATIENTS ON DEMAND

From the Founder & CEO of mLive Software

# PATIENTS ON DEMAND

5 Steps to a Steady Stream of Patients
for Your Dental Practice in a **Digital-First**,
**Post-Pandemic** World

## ADAM WITTY

Published by Advantage, Charleston, South Carolina.
Member of Advantage Media Group.

ADVANTAGE is a registered trademark, and the Advantage colophon is a trademark of Advantage Media Group, Inc.

Printed in the United States of America.

10 9 8 7 6 5 4 3 2 1

ISBN: 978-1-64225-281-1
LCCN: 2021932207

Cover design by Katie Biondo.

This publication is designed to provide accurate and authoritative information in regard to the subject matter covered. It is sold with the understanding that the publisher is not engaged in rendering legal, accounting, or other professional services. If legal advice or other expert assistance is required, the services of a competent professional person should be sought.

Advantage Media Group is proud to be a part of the Tree Neutral® program. Tree Neutral offsets the number of trees consumed in the production and printing of this book by taking proactive steps such as planting trees in direct proportion to the number of trees used to print books. To learn more about Tree Neutral, please visit **www.treeneutral.com**.

Advantage Media Group is a publisher of business, self-improvement, and professional development books and online learning. We help entrepreneurs, business leaders, and professionals share their Stories, Passion, and Knowledge to help others Learn & Grow. Do you have a manuscript or book idea that you would like us to consider for publishing? Please visit **advantagefamily.com** or call **1.843.414.5600**.

# CONTENTS

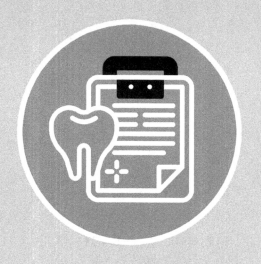

### CHAPTER 1

# BATTEN DOWN THE HATCHES

*The Outside Disruptive Forces*
*Hurled upon Dentistry*

I want to talk about some of the challenges in dentistry. I never want to start a book on a negative note, but we need to acknowledge the reality doctors are facing. Facts and data are key.

What general dentists face today is dire in many regards. If you don't take things into your own hands, you are leaving your fate to others.

## DOCTOR TAKE-HOME PAY IS DROPPING BY $3K PER YEAR

Since 2005, year-over-year take-home pay of the average general dentist in America has gone down. Income has dropped from an average of $219,000 in 2005 to $174,000 today. That's a drop of almost $3,000 per year! Of course there are myriad reasons behind the drop, and we don't have time to debate all of those reasons, but facts are facts. The average doctor is taking home less money every year from their practice. This is something to be worried about.

## THE AVERAGE RETIREMENT AGE FOR A DOCTOR IS INCREASING BY SIX MONTHS PER YEAR

The second sobering statistic, and this ties directly with the above, is that the average age of retirement for a doctor has gone up by six years over the last thirteen years. Doctors are making less and less, and because of that they are forced to work longer.

*The average doctor is taking home less money every year from their practice. This is something to be worried about.*

## INSURANCE-RELATED REIMBURSEMENTS HAVE DECLINED BY 27 PERCENT

Every doctor knows about insurance and managed care and the nightmare and mess all of that is. It means doctors are getting paid less for the services they deliver to patients each day. Reimbursements have dropped 27 percent over the last ten years. As more pressure is placed on general dentists you will see that trend continue. We have politicians in Washington that believe healthcare should be free. We have politicians in Washington that believe the government should control healthcare. I have no interest in political debates. We all know that if the government is in charge of healthcare, reimbursements will continue to get smaller.

## OPERATING OVERHEAD GROWS TO AN INDUSTRY HIGH

Operating overhead in your practice has also risen. Fifty percent overhead was the norm a decade ago. Today general practice overhead averages 65 percent. It is more expensive today to operate a practice than at any other time. It's more expensive to hire people. It's more expensive when an employee doesn't make it and they need to exit your practice. Rent is more expensive. Equipment is more expensive. Costs are going up and reimbursements are going down. This combination is a terrible elixir for any doctor.

## CORPORATE DENTISTRY IS PROJECTED TO GROW

I don't think I need to say anything about corporate dentistry. You are all too aware. It is rapidly expanding and taking over a good chunk of the general dentistry market in the United States. Every independent, entrepreneurial doctor needs to be aware that corporate dentistry will drive prices down. By 2036 it is estimated that half (50 percent) of all general practices in America will be corporate owned.

## PRACTICE VALUES ARE DECLINING

What does all of this mean for you as a doctor? It means the value of your practice is going down. You've spent your entire life becoming educated and building a practice of your own. You have earned income from your practice each year. You also have equity value in your practice when you retire and sell. Incomes are going down and practice values are going down. When all is said and done and you are ready to hang it up and retire, your practice will likely be worth less.

This is something that you should be concerned about. There is *so* much outside pressure on general dentists in America. You don't have to sit here and throw your hands in the air. Action can be taken. This book will give you a plan for prosperity, a plan for creating *patients on demand*. Unless you are willing to fight back and take action, it's a pretty grim story.

# NOTES

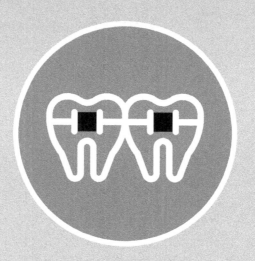

### CHAPTER 2

# WELCOME TO A DIGITAL-FIRST, POST-PANDEMIC ECONOMY

*How COVID Has Transformed Patient Research, Shopping, and Buying More in Nine Months Than the Previous Ten Years*

W elcome to the digital-first, post-pandemic economy.

As Charles Darwin said, "It isn't the strongest that survives but the most adaptable to change."

We are now living in a *new world*, a *new digital economy*.

As a practice owner, understanding how to adapt and thrive in this new digital-first, post-pandemic world is *your number-one job*.

I'll start with a staggering statistic from our friends at the US Department of Commerce. In just sixty days, *e-commerce has grown more than it had in the past decade*. Ignoring this opportunity could be deadly to your practice.

Since the beginning of the COVID-19 pandemic in the United States in early March 2020, America (and the world) has shifted from offline to online at a dizzying pace. It was as if someone had dropped a cement block on an accelerator pedal.

Since 2009, over the last eleven years, e-commerce adoption has grown about 1 percent to 2 percent per year. In other words, the percentage of people that do their primary shopping online versus offline is growing.

*In just sixty days, e-commerce has grown more than it had in the past decade. Ignoring this opportunity could be deadly to your practice.*

The general practice doctor might say, "Gee, Adam, my patients have to come into my practice to receive care, so this doesn't really apply to me." While that may be true, this is *very* relevant to you because of how your patients shop. Your patients and prospects conduct all of their research and prepurchase investigation online. If your practice doesn't have an impressive digital presence, you're going to get left behind.

## E-COMMERCE HAS GROWN MORE IN TWO MONTHS THAN IT HAS IN THE PAST 10 YEARS

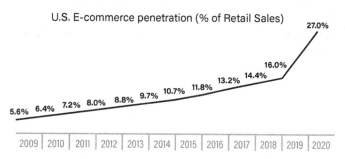

U.S. E-commerce penetration (% of Retail Sales)

| 2009 | 2010 | 2011 | 2012 | 2013 | 2014 | 2015 | 2016 | 2017 | 2018 | 2019 | 2020 |
|------|------|------|------|------|------|------|------|------|------|------|------|
| 5.6% | 6.4% | 7.2% | 8.0% | 8.8% | 9.7% | 10.7% | 11.8% | 13.2% | 14.4% | 16.0% | 27.0% |

Source: Bank of America, U.S. Department of Commerce, Shawspring Research, Forbes.com

As new, COVID-induced online purchase patterns now become habits, experts expect that online commerce, marketing, and sales will continue a rapid climb with further adoption.

The next statistic I will share comes from the NASDAQ stock index and business television network CNBC. Six "tech" companies (Apple, Microsoft, Amazon, Facebook, Alphabet [Google], and Tesla) now have a combined value that is almost equivalent to the other ninety-four "Top 100" companies listed on NASDAQ.

COVID is accelerating people's push to online, digital, and tech and, as a result, skyrocketing the value of these companies.

## NASDAQ 100: BIGGEST STOCKS

Share of total index, weighted by market cap

| ALL OTHERS 51.0% | APPLE 12.0% | FACEBOOK 4.2% |
| | MICROSOFT 11.3% | ALPHABET (Cl A) 3.8% |
| | | ALPHABET (Cl B) 3.8% |
| | AMAZON 11.2% | TESLA 2.7% |

Source: FactSet

You can't fight it. It is what it is. The trend is going to continue. Instead, you can embrace the trend and be ahead of the wave and take advantage of the opportunities that are coming. Before we do that, we must cover the five biggest marketing mistakes that practice owners make each and every day. Pay close attention and you will see how a digital-first, post-pandemic world only magnifies these mistakes to make their impact more deadly.

# NOTES

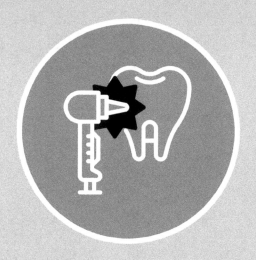

### CHAPTER 3

# YOU ARE YOUR OWN WORST ENEMY

*The Five Biggest Marketing
Mistakes Practices Make and How
COVID Has Magnified Them*

E very entrepreneur makes mistakes. Don't beat
yourself up. Successful entrepreneurs *learn* from
their mistakes and change.

Over the last fifteen years, I've had the opportunity to work with a few hundred general dentists. My
work was always focused upon helping the doctor more
clearly and efficiently market themself to magnetically

attract new patients to their practice.

Having "looked under the hood" of so many practices, I found lots of mistakes. Despite the hundreds I found, I saw distinct patterns and commonalities. If all you do is correct one of the five following most common mistakes, you will have a remarkably better practice. So what are they?

## LOOKS LIKE, SMELLS LIKE, ACTS LIKE A COMMODITY

As a consumer, do you buy the highest-priced commodity (say gasoline) or the lowest-priced commodity? The answer is simple: *all* consumers purchase commodities by price, and the lowest price always prevails. You've probably been guilty a time or two of driving an extra mile down the road to save a few pennies per gallon on the price of gasoline. When it all appears to be the same, why would you pay anything above the lowest possible price?

Having worked with hundreds of practices, I can make *this* definitive statement: with a few exceptions, most practices look, smell, and act the same. "Fitting in" seems to be a trait exhibited by most dentists.

Perhaps it was encouraged in school? Doctors, perhaps unconsciously, work extra hard to create an office environment, suite of treatments, and pricing that is similar to most other practices. In doing so doctors place themselves and their practice in a dangerous trap.

When your practice is similar to most any other, your patients will make their treatment decisions based on price

> *When it all appears to be the same, why would you pay anything above the lowest possible price?*

(lowest) and location (closest to their home or office). Not much else will matter.

## NO CONSISTENT COMMUNICATION WITH PROSPECTS/PATIENTS AND LEADS

Most doctors I meet are "reluctant" entrepreneurs. In other words, they love treating patients and hate running a business. This partially explains why corporate dentistry is expected to grow to 50 percent of all practices by 2036. As a reluctant entrepreneur, most doctors don't do the things that successful entrepreneurs do. Namely, they don't communicate consistently with prospects and patients.

Successful entrepreneurs know that the large majority of prospects aren't ready to buy their product or service immediately. They know they must "nurture" the prospect. They know that the best form of nurturing is consistent communication. In other words, staying in regular touch with your prospects and patients will do more to grow your practice than anything else. Because most doctors would rather perform clinical treatment than communicate with patients, guess what? Communication never happens!

## TRANSACTION-MINDED, NOT RELATIONSHIP-MINDED

Where does all the value in a dental practice live? Not in your office, fancy machines, or your exquisite clinical care. All equity value in your practices lies within your patients. Specifically, the lifetime value of your patients and the quality of relationship your practice has with your patients. *Any* business is nothing more than the sum of the value of the relationships it has with its customers.

*Any business is nothing more than the sum of the value of the relationships it has with its customers.*

Let us consider two businesses that you are likely familiar with. The first is Blockbuster. While not around anymore, I suspect you might have been a customer years before. Blockbuster treated you like a transaction. Every time you came into the store to rent a movie, you would pull out your wallet, Blockbuster would swipe your credit card, and they would instruct you to return the movie within forty-eight hours or face stiff late fees. Not until the near end did Blockbuster even collect consumer information, and they never made recommendations based upon your previous rental history. Blockbuster declared bankruptcy in 2010 and ceased operations. Blockbuster was a transaction-minded business.

Now, let us consider Netflix. As of 2020, Netflix had 195 million Members that pay an average of $9.99 per month for unlimited video streaming services. Unlike Blockbuster, Netflix has a record of every movie/video you've ever watched. Because of this, it makes intelligent recommendations of new movies or shows that will pique your interest. Furthermore, Netflix has invested billions of dollars in creating original content with the goal of adding more value to

Members and extending the lifetime value (and satisfaction) of a Member. Netflix is a relationship-minded business and they have been handsomely rewarded. As of this writing (2021), Netflix has a market value of $260 billion dollars.

As the doctor (a.k.a. the boss), you get to decide. Your practice can be transaction-minded or your practice can be relationship-minded. You can be Blockbuster or you can be Netflix. You get to decide.

## LITTLE TO NO FOLLOW-UP

According to the National Sales Executive Association, 80 percent of all sales are made between the fifth and twelfth contact with a prospect. Yes, I know, your practice needs *new patients now*. I hear you. Remember what I said just a few moments ago. The large majority of prospects aren't ready to buy your treatment immediately. They need to be nurtured. If you are only looking for immediate buyers, like an addict hooked on

*As the doctor (a.k.a. the boss), you get to decide. Your practice can be transaction-minded or your practice can be relationship-minded.*

cocaine, you will burn through 90 to 95 percent of your leads. Combine this with the fact that it takes an average of five-plus contacts before a prospect is ready to buy.

In the hundreds of practices I've worked with, rarely do I see a follow-up system to capture the value of their prospect leads. Here is what the typical practice looks like. Brenda is working at your front desk. An email from a prospect comes through your website. Brenda courteously replies to the prospect inviting him or her to schedule an appointment. Brenda does not get a reply. Brenda has moved her attention to other priorities and forgotten about the prospect. The prospect received one email from Brenda and that is it. No other follow-up occurs. You flush your hard-earned money down the commode.

## NO AUTOMATION, NO SYSTEMS, NO PROCESSES

What keeps most practices small and many living hand-to-mouth? No systems, no processes, no automation. Most things in the practice are manual (at least marketing) and one-off. When everything is manual, balls drop, details slip, and humans fail.

I talked a moment ago about Blockbuster and Netflix. Another *big* differentiator is Netflix's reliance on automation. Algorithms and automation make it easy for Netflix to automatically recommend movies and shows you will like. At Blockbuster, most everything was manual. The same is true in a practice. The embrace and adoption of marketing automation gives you the opportunity to build meaningful relationships with prospects and patients at scale.

Every practice owner should be thinking about how to talk to your patients, how to strengthen relationships, and how to solidify the culture of your practice, now more than ever.

In the next chapter I lay out my five simple, easy-to-implement steps that will help your practice compete and win in a digital-first, post-pandemic world.

# NOTES

# NOTES

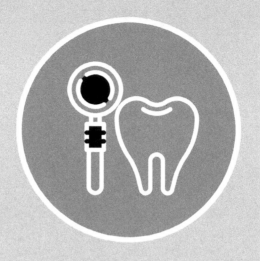

### CHAPTER 4

# PATIENTS ON DEMAND

*Your Five-Step Battle Plan to Thwart These Negative Forces and Create a Steady Stream of Patients for Your Practice*

## #1: ESTABLISH YOUR DIFFERENTIATION FACTORS, BUILD VALUE WITH YOUR EXISTING PATIENTS, FOCUS ON QUALITY OVER QUANTITY

The hardest thing in business is to get a customer. In your case, the hardest thing in your practice is to get a patient. Most doctors don't appreciate and recognize how hard it is to get a new patient to walk through the door. When you realize the hardest thing in your practice is getting a new patient, the amount of time and energy that you invest into nurturing your existing patient relationships will change significantly.

There are so many choices in the marketplace today, and dentistry is no different. If you think about the brand of bread you're going to purchase at the supermarket or what TV program you'll tune into tonight, consumers are overwhelmed by choice. When overwhelmed, we make the choice easier in our minds by attempting to commoditize that purchase, or we see all choices as mostly the same. When you are seen as a commodity, it is easier for the patient to choose, because any option will do. You are substitutable. When everything looks and sounds the same, when it is an "apples to apples" comparison, what do we purchase on? Every commodity is purchased on price, and it's not the highest price that is purchased, it's the lowest price. You must realize that your prospective patients *want* to view you as a commodity, because it makes their purchase decision easier. The biggest thing that you can do as a doctor is not let you and your practice get put in the commodity trap. Don't allow a patient or a prospect to see or think for one second that you're just like everybody else.

One of my favorite books is *Almost Alchemy* by marketing legend Dan Kennedy. The premise of the book and the subtitle is *How to Get More from Fewer and Less*. In this

> *The biggest thing that you can do as a doctor is not let you and your practice get put in the commodity trap.*

book, the central argument Dan Kennedy makes is that as time goes on, it will be harder and harder to get customers, and in order to not only survive but thrive you've gotta do more business with the customers (patients) you already have. The way you do more business and the way you charge more for the business you do is by being different. To create value, you must be different. If you look like, sound like, and smell like everybody else, you're a commodity, and consumers always buy the lowest-priced commodity. To create value, your practice must be different and do what your competitors largely ignore. Your fellow doctors largely ignore the importance of building relationships with patients.

In dentistry, most think about price, insurance, convenience, etc. Don't fall into this trap. Take out a piece of paper. Fold it in half. Unfold it, and on the left side of the crease, write "My Practice." On the right side of the crease, write "Other Practices." On the left write all the ways that you want to differentiate yourself and your practice. Look at what other practices are doing and determine what you can do to take your practice to the next level.

You must be the clear choice in your prospective patient's mind and you must remain the clear choice in your existing patient's mind. Don't for a minute take your patients for granted and think that they won't leave you. If you don't invest in nurturing relationships with your patients they will graze off to greener pastures. Ask yourself, what is my practice doing to differentiate while simultaneously protecting and building value with existing patients so my practice is the clear choice?

Do you realize in dentistry there are a lot more patients that we don't get than the patients we do get? What's happening on the periphery, the external, all the people that never make it through a phone call to appointment or through the door from consultation to treatment? That's the real business! That's the difference between waiting for people to show up (which most dentists do!) and taking control of cultivating your patient relationships.

Success is largely doing the exact opposite of what the masses are doing. Most dental practices are not building relationships. They are not creating value. They are not distinguishing and differentiating themselves. When you invest time and energy into this it puts you and your practice into a category of one.

> *Success is largely doing the exact opposite of what the masses are doing.*

## #2: BE MORE RELATIONSHIP-DRIVEN AND LESS DENTAL-DRIVEN WITH NO-FAIL, MULTISTEP FOLLOW-UP

The future of dentistry still includes people. In fact, the constant that will always exist in our lives and practices is the people. Now is our chance to be less dental, less clinical, less commodity-driven, and more relationship-driven. You must practice relationship-based dentistry.

Some call it comprehensive dentistry. What can you and your practice do to further your relationships with patients right now?

Most dentists I talk to want a beautiful life. They want a good balance between their practice and personal life. They want a real practice, one that is self-managed. If you want to look forward to waking up every morning and walking into your practice, then you must become more relationship-driven and less dental-driven. At the end of the day, you can't practice without patients, and they can't be patients without you. Double down on patient relationships.

When I speak at dental conferences, I ask this question: "Is your practice built on a foundation of sand, or is your practice built on a foundation of bedrock?" A practice built on a foundation of sand is one that is transaction-focused. Patients come in your door, they get a cleaning or other one-off dental procedure, and then you rush them out so you can make room in the chair for the next patient. When the patient is due for their next cleaning or they need something else, you hope they will come back to you. That's a transaction-based practice, one that sits on a foundation of sand.

A relationship-based practice is built on a foundation of bedrock.

If your practice is built on a foundation of bedrock, a foundation of quality patient relationships, then your practice will be secure. When you have strong relationships with your patients, no matter what happens, they're not leaving your practice. They're not leaving you. They're like a part of your family. They're not going to turn their back on you when times turn bad. There will be bad times in the life of

> *If your practice is built on a foundation of bedrock, a foundation of quality patient relationships, then your practice will be secure.*

your practice. For all practices it was COVID-19. In truth, there will be another bad time that will come at some point in the future. When times are good, it's easy. When times are good, practices are making money hand over fist. But when the tide goes out, we're going to discover which practices have been "skinny dipping" and only addressing patient relationships on the surface. Practices built upon a foundation of sand are decimated when the storms come.

People buy people, they don't buy practices. Who do you buy from? You buy from people you know, like, and trust. Most importantly you buy from people with whom you have a relationship. When you have a relationship with someone, you feel guilty turning your back on them or their business. When no relationship exists and it's a transaction, they can take it or leave it. If the next practice is more convenient, closer to their house, cheaper, easier, you name it, then they will move on to the next dentist.

Patients don't buy the highest education. If you went to Harvard, great, but that's not why patients buy from you. Patients don't buy from you because of your fancy, cutting-edge equipment. Investing in the latest, greatest, fancy technology equipment is neat, but that's not why patients buy from you. And it's not because you have the nicest office. A nice office is expected, it's not the reason that a patient chooses to get their care from you. The reason people choose you is ultimately because of the relationship. Now more than ever, relationships that you have with your patients are the essence of having a practice built upon a foundation of bedrock.

What can you do to expand, strengthen, and deepen the relationship you have with your patients? How can you build greater attachment to you and your practice? What are you doing when the patient isn't in front of you? I know what happens when the patient is in front of you, but what are you doing when the patient isn't? What are you doing to branch out and expand that relationship to patients that you don't get into the chair? How can you flip more referral opportunities? How can you be more personable, more authentic, more genuine? The practice that shows up the most makes the most money, end of story. The doctor that shows up the most deals with the best patients, gets the greatest value, and gets the most referrals.

You must have a systematic approach that allows you to cast a bigger net so you're dealing with more than just the people that are already in the chair.

**The practice that shows up the most makes the most money, end of story.**

## #3: CREATE CONNECTION WITH YOUR COMMUNITY

How good does it feel that much of your practice is what we would call event-driven and emergency-driven dentistry? In other words, you are at the mercy of people being in pain and in poor health. Not good. You are at the mercy of an incident and really have no control.

It doesn't have to be this way.

In dentistry, it's about what you are doing to connect with your community so patients have more opportunities to refer and more opportunities to be educated by you. If you create a connection with your community, you are setting the rules, you are determining what health is, you are defining the way that patients interact with you and how they value and view dentistry. Many practices are desperate for "the next patient." They are more desperate than ever. If you focus on the community, you don't have to be desperate.

Very few doctors see themselves as having a community. The majority say, "I've got patients, and a patient is a number on a spreadsheet. I've got two thousand patients!" And when you treat people as such, simply a patient who's a name and number on a spreadsheet, then they are going to treat you equally.

When times get tough, they're gone. When a new dental office opens closer to their home, they're gone. When they need something more sophisticated than you can provide, they go straight to the provider without seeking your counsel.

Here is your measuring stick to determine how well your practice is doing:

- What is the average lifetime value of a patient to your practice? You should be able to answer that question immediately. It should be a key performance indicator (KPI) you see regularly.

- What is the average number of people a patient refers to your practice over their lifetime?

We all know and agree that the best new patients are referrals from existing patients. When I ask doctors, "What's the best method for getting new patients into your practice," they all say referrals. That's what I would say too. And they are. Most practices don't even know how many people an engaged patient will refer over their lifetime.

You must build relationships. You must proactively communicate with your patients. You must communicate to drive engagement. You want your patients to reply to your emails. You want your patients to send questions to you. You want to have conversations with your patients. You must create points of connection with your patients. If you weld the patients to you, then they won't go anywhere else.

## #4: CONSISTENTLY SHARE EDUCATIONAL CONTENT SO PATIENTS SEE YOU AS THE AUTHORITY AND GO-TO EXPERT

Consistently is a very important word. If you're building a practice in a healthy profit-based way, you'll win every time as long as you do it *consistently*. But the thing we don't talk about often enough is that there has to be continuity: you can't have a gap. So your only fear would be, *if it's not important to go to the dentist right now, for fear of the virus, why would it ever be important?* If we can wait a month, why can't we wait two? Why can't we wait

> *If you weld the patients to you, then they won't go anywhere else.*

three? If I had one cleaning this year, and I'm okay because we had a little shutdown, well maybe I can do once-a-year from now on? The gap in the mind is closed by continuously feeding people the right way of thinking.

If you give them the guidance on how to make decisions, you will control those decisions. This is very important because every doctor will get what you are willing to accept. The patient will respond and make their decisions based upon what you educate them to do. By sharing helpful content and educational information, educating nonstop, you greatly influence (control really) the patient's decision. You don't have to sell. You just have to *educate*. How do you help your patients make a smart decision? If we're not sharing helpful and educational material consistently, then we are not influencing (controlling), and therefore their lack of treatment is our fault, not the patient's.

Your identity is not a doctor. It's bigger than that. You also are a business owner. You might also be a husband, wife, father, or mother. You are also a leader and teacher. You have an opportunity to advise your patients as the authority with go-to-expert positioning. If you do this continuously, you have the ability to build a bigger vision and image of yourself in the mind of your prospective and existing patients and thereby supercharge the patient value and their desire to refer others to you. *Think of yourself as an educator first and a doctor second.*

The greatest marketing lesson I ever learned was something called CTI: Customer Time Invested. It's a very simple principle. The more time a prospect invests in learning about you, reading about you, consuming information that is published by you or shared by you, the more likely they are to

> *Think of yourself as an educator first and a doctor second.*

purchase from you. If they're an existing patient, the more likely they are to stay and never go anywhere else. So what does that mean? It means you've got to give people content and information that's helpful to them. You've gotta help your patients make smarter decisions. No one wants to make a bad decision. It's your job to educate them and to help them make better decisions. The more content that you publish, the more content you share with your community, and the more consumer time that they invest in consuming your content, then the more of an authority you become to them. The higher up in income you go, the more you are paid for *who you are* rather than *what you do*.

There are plenty of dentists that have personal income over $500,000 a year. There are plenty of dentists that have personal income of less than $100,000 a year. How could two people that do the same thing earn such different incomes? The doctor that earns five times the income of their peer is a bigger *who*. To build your income you must build your who. People will pay more money to work with the doctor that *shows up the most* and is seen as an authority and go-to expert in their field. You must provide patients and prospects more content and information that's helpful to them so they can make smarter decisions.

> *The higher up in income you go, the more you are paid for who you are rather than what you do.*

How do you do it? You publish a monthly news-letter, print or digital. Every month you drip content to them. They see your content. They consume your content. You send timely and helpful content-based emails. You think about writing and publishing a book. Then you take that book and turn it into articles and special reports and white papers.

I want to share a quick story. My dentist is my former next-door neighbor. Many of you may have a next-door neighbor that is a patient too. Unless you own multiple homes or move often, the "next-door neighbor as patient" angle is usually good for just one or two patients. I went to see Dr. Phillips because he was my next-door neighbor. I liked him. I knew him. I trusted him. I felt like *he and I had a relationship* because he'd invite my wife Erin and I over to his house for a barbecue in the backyard. There was a genuine relationship.

Dr. Phillips sold his practice two years ago. The doctor he sold to is a nice guy. In the two years since Dr. Phillips sold his practice I've continued to be a patient of the new doctor. In those two years there has never been any proactive communication. Not once has there been any proactive relationship building. The doctor he sold to was just a doctor. He became a commodity to me. I didn't feel I had any relationship with him. He wasn't giving me any content to consume or educating me. He wasn't communicating with me in any way. He wasn't building a relationship. So … I decided to try another doctor. I decided to try another doctor that was pro-actively building relationships with patients. Building authority and creating content that your patients want is one of the top things you must do to create genuine patient relationships that allow you to build a practice on a foundation of bedrock and not on sand.

## #5: AUTOMATION AND SYSTEMS

You went to school to be a dentist, not a marketer. Yet being a dental practice owner puts you in the marketing business, whether you like it or not! There is a dirty little secret most don't want you to know. *You can grow your practice with good marketing without being a marketing expert.* To compensate for your marketing weakness you must have automation and systems that do the work for you.

> *You can grow your practice with good marketing without being a marketing expert.*

The first company I worked for as a young lad while still in high school kept their customer list on a rolodex in the sales manager's office. Marketing was done by advertising in trade journals and print magazines. This company had no ongoing communication or nurturing of existing customers with the exception of a promotional flyer included in product orders shipped from their warehouse. *Like most businesses, they just expected their customers to keep coming back*. This is a *dangerous* assumption.

Today, it has never been easier to browse, shop, and search for alternative products and providers. As mentioned earlier, online browsing and shopping has grown more in the past two months than the previous ten years combined. This is both a *threat* and an *opportunity*.

When I started my first business in 2005, I invested in Salesforce.com. A web-based customer relationship management system, Salesforce was an easy way for our marketing and sales team to keep track of every single customer. The software allowed us to easily update contact information, view purchase history, and log all communication between our business and the customer. This software not only allowed us to track customer communication but also automated most all of it for us. Automation and systems allowed me to scale my first business from $2M to over $20M in four short years.

I realize you may not want a multi-location $20M revenue practice. Scale and growth may *not* be your top priority. That is all fine and well. While you may not want that, I bet (and hope) you want a steady stream of patients into your practice each week, month, and year. To implement steps one through four you must have automation and systems or it will fail.

The secret I'm about to share is the single greatest way to maximize and move your practice to a higher level of sophistication and strength within your patient base and community. Equally important, it will attract new patients to you who have the ability to buy.

After all of this COVID mess, are you going to be stronger than your peers? One in four small businesses will close their doors for good when COVID fully shakes out and has passed. There will be lots of practices that are feeble and weak. My job is to make sure you are strong and positioned to take advantage of the opportunity that this digital-first, post-pandemic economy is creating.

Over the years, I've come to understand the pain points every dentist experiences when it comes to marketing themselves, marketing their practice, and creating genuine patient relationships. My first business, Advantage|ForbesBooks, has served hundreds of dentists. My second business, Magnetic Marketing, proudly has hundreds of dentists as active Members in a thriving community. I've come to know dentistry, dentists, and the things that keep you awake at night.

In 2001, Steve Jobs had a big idea. It was revolutionary, and it revolutionized an industry and ultimately changed the world. Steve Jobs's big idea was "*a thousand songs in your pocket.*" My big idea is *modern dental marketing and patient relationship marketing with a high-tech personal feel that gives every dentist the equivalent of a full-time marketing team for a tiny fraction of the price.*

I'll tell you about my new business that supports dentists in the next chapter.

# NOTES

# NOTES

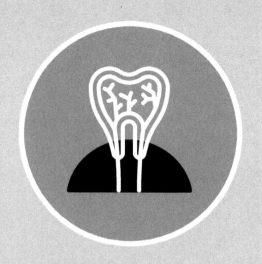

# END YOUR MARKETING FRUSTRATIONS FOR GOOD

On November 19, 2019, I married the woman of my dreams. She later told me my smile was one of the first things that caught her eye. Without fabulous dental care throughout my life, my smile might not have made the cut.

A beautiful smile is a *life giver*. When a person has a great smile, they are more confident, they are more likely to attract a partner, they are more likely to be eligible for promotion or advancement. Simply put, a great smile is an accelerant to success. You and your practice make a positive difference in the lives of thousands of patients each and every day.

If only you could create a steady stream of patients for your practice. Not only would you and your practice be better off, but the lives of those patients would be too. More patients are better for you and better for the patient.

Like you, I am an entrepreneur, a business owner, a person responsible for the livelihood of my team members. I know what it is like to meet payroll, figure out marketing, and deliver for customers daily while keeping enough money flowing in to meet all obligations and have something left over at the end of the day.

*If only you could create a steady stream of patients for your practice. Not only would you and your practice be better off, but the lives of those patients would be too.*

I also know that figuring out the marketing puzzle is the hardest thing in business. In fact, more businesses (including dental practices) close their doors because of the inability to generate a steady and sufficient stream of new customers (patients) to keep the doors open.

For the past fifteen years, all of my businesses have been focused on helping entrepreneurs improve their marketing which in turn improves their business. Our Core Purpose is *Growing Entrepreneurs and Businesses to Benefit All Mankind.*

After working with hundreds of practices over the last fifteen years, I started a new business in 2020 to solve the many problems I shared in this book.

## MLIVE IS A NEW PATIENT MARKETING AUTOMATION PLATFORM FOR DENTISTS

mLive is a fully automated, turnkey marketing platform that continuously builds relationships with your patients and prospects through multistep marketing.

mLive features a massive library of multistep marketing campaigns for general dentists that are building relationships and attracting new patients into their practice. And we have a team of marketers, copywriters, graphic designers, and technologists that are working each and every day to build new multistep campaigns that get inserted into the mLive library every single month.

When you become a Member of mLive, you receive access to new custom marketing campaigns that you can use for your practice each and every month. Every campaign that we create is multistep, with five to fifteen different steps! You're leading with educational information for patients and prospects.

mLive accomplishes five big things for dental practices:

1.  Automates the process of attracting quality new patient leads to your practice.

2.  Motivates and converts new patients into lifetime patients, increasing patient lifetime value, a metric every doctor should be tracking.

3.  Engages and retains existing patients to become more valuable through additional purchased services. They come to you for new forms of treatment. They also refer and bring new patients into your practice.

4.  Creates a referral machine in your practice.

How do you increase the quantity and quality of the referrals that your patients are giving you? You build a relationship with your patients!

5. Automates your practice and makes it easier for you to run a successful practice.

## WHAT IS MARKETING AUTOMATION?

Why do a few practices grow while the majority do not? What do the top few have in common? They've deployed *marketing automation* inside their practice. They recognize a fundamental principle: *technology that educates prospects and patients will yield new, better, and more patients for their practice automatically.*

With marketing automation, dentists can spend more time with patients chairside while technology delivers new patients that pay, stay, and refer.

**Au-to-ma-tion:** Technology by which a process or procedure is performed with minimal human assistance

## MARKETING AUTOMATION DEFINED

Marketing automation is *technology that manages marketing processes and campaigns*, across multiple channels, automatically to *increase revenue and maximize efficiency* while *limiting the amount of human input needed*.

Let's dissect this definition.

**Technology that manages marketing processes and campaigns**. Science and data show that multistep, multichannel campaigns yield the highest response and ROI. Manually executing a five- to fifteen-step marketing campaign is grueling and time consuming. Most practices waste marketing dollars because they lack follow-up. Marketing automation makes follow-up easy.

**Increase revenue and maximize efficiency**. The average general practice is stagnant. Revenues are flat.

Marketing automation allows you to reach thousands of prospects and patients with highly valuable content and education that positions you as the authority and preconditions them to accept treatment. All of this with the click of a button.

**Limiting the amount of human input needed**. General practices are overworked and maxed out. The doctor needs to spend time chairside delivering outstanding clinical care. The staff needs to schedule and coordinate a beautiful patient experience. Who has time for marketing? Marketing automation allows you to accomplish hours of marketing in minutes.

*Marketing automation allows you to reach thousands of prospects and patients with highly valuable content and education that positions you as the authority and preconditions them to accept treatment.*

## MARKETING AUTOMATION IS YOUR SECRET WEAPON

The average general practice in America generates $771K in annual revenue. Very few exceed $1M. The $1M+ practices don't necessarily provide better clinical care, but they do market more effectively. $1M+ practices use marketing systems and technology that *automate* the mundane (but necessary) process of attracting, converting, and retaining patients. $1M+ practices rely on technology (with human guidance) to do the heavy lifting. Practice growth and prosperity can be achieved in any practice. Marketing automation is a key ingredient.

## HOW DO YOU CREATE PATIENTS ON DEMAND?

Allow us to introduce you to the Marketing Automation Coliseum. Just like the Colosseum in Rome that is almost two thousand years old, our Marketing Automation Coliseum is built on a solid foundation of *automation and done-for you.* The Coliseum reliably and automatically creates new and better patients for your practice on autopilot.

Without technology to automate, the manual to-dos will overwhelm your team and won't get done. Without prebuilt, multistep campaigns you won't have time to write copy, design ads and landing pages, and assemble all the pieces. mLive software does all the heavy lifting. mLive's exceptional team of direct response marketers build ready-to-deploy campaigns that are carefully crafted to generate response.

What are the four pillars to the Coliseum that generate a steady stream of patients?

## Communicate and Educate

Doctors must reliably and consistently communicate and educate prospects and patients. As the expert and authority (you have a Dr. in front of your name!), you must lead patients to the treatment options that serve them best. Rather than *pushing* prospects to your practice through advertising, data shows *pulling* prospects to you with educational content performs best.

## Nurture and Follow Up

On average, a prospect must be communicated or engaged with at least five times prior to a purchase. Most marketing dollars are wasted because of limited follow-up. No-fail, follow-up marketing that nurtures relationships is part of mLive.

## Build Relationships and Community

The greatest source of new patients to any dental practice are referrals. Unfortunately, most doctors practice "transactional-medicine" rather than "relationship-medicine." By continually educating patients, by proactively communicating with them every month, you deepen patient relationships and create a patient community that is motivated and inspired to refer.

## Upsell, Cross Sell, and Next Sell

While most practices are squarely focused on new patients, successful practices know that increasing the lifetime value of an existing patient is an easier path for growth and profit. Few practices know their lifetime patient value (LPV). mLive educates existing patients about new treatment options and services you offer to illicit interest and generate internal appointments.

## OUTCOMES OF MARKETING AUTOMATION

### Lead Generation

With marketing automation, your practice will attract higher quality and quantity new patient leads. mLive content and education provides a magnetic pull, creating interest in place of resistance. Given the choice, patients prefer to select the doctor and practice that is *pulling* them with education rather than *pushing* them with ads.

### Lead to Patient Conversion

No trust = No sale. If the prospect doesn't trust you and your practice, they will not accept treatment. If you don't follow up, they will quickly forget

> *Given the choice, patients prefer to select the doctor and practice that is pulling them with education rather than pushing them with ads.*

about you. If you look like every other practice in your community, they will see you as a commodity and buy the lowest price. mLive's automated multistep patient education and follow-up builds your credibility and keeps you "top of mind" with prospects.

## Patient Retention and Referrals

Retaining patients to increase lifetime patient value (LPV) and having them refer friends and family is paramount to practice growth. You must focus on relationships rather than transactions. You must build a community that patients are proud to be part of. If patients don't hear from you, learn from you, and take your advice they will look elsewhere. Genuine relationships inspire referrals and introductions.

# WHAT IS MULTISTEP MARKETING?

Multistep marketing is the combination of messages sent to your prospective patients in a series in many different versions to capture their attention. Said differently, it is making sure your message is seen everywhere in a short period of time: social media, website, landing pages, email, etc. The combination of different channels is what makes multistep marketing better than anything else.

*Eighty percent of sales conversions are made after the fifth contact.* If you have two thousand patients and maybe two hundred prospects on top of that you now have to send each of these multistep campaigns to each patient. This is extremely time-consuming! Because of the time and money most practice owners don't do a good job of proactively marketing their practice. This is why most practices are built on a foundation of sand rather than bedrock.

*Eighty percent of sales conversions are made after the fifth contact.*

Most practices invest all of this time and money generating leads, and 90 percent of the money you spend to generate all of these prospective patients you wash down the drain because after two attempts you say, "Oh, they're not interested." The majority of the leads you generate are "suspects." They are not really prospects because they never pick up the phone and they never answer your call. You never make a real effort to go after them, to stay in touch with them, to build a relationship with them, to communicate with them.

## WHAT IS MY INVESTMENT?

In our research, we identified two big reasons why most practice owners don't invest in marketing. First, it is expensive. If you want to have a dental marketing agency do it all for you, this is a $10,000 to $15,000 per month investment. When I say marketing, I don't mean a banner ad that you put on Facebook. I mean integrated, multistep campaigns with five to fifteen different steps that take the prospect through an educational funnel that prepares them to buy and then converts them into patients. Most dentists just aren't able to invest $10,000 to $15,000 per month in custom dental marketing campaigns for their practice. The other big reason most practices don't market is the time commitment. Of course, you can hire a marketing coordinator to *implement* all the work your dental marketing agency produced. That will cost you another $4,000 to $5,000 per month.

For as little as the price of just two new patients a year to your practice, you can have a fully automated and managed system that generates new patients. It's inexpensive at $997 a month, which is a fraction of the cost of having a marketing person on your team. If you hire a marketing agency to do all this for you, you'd spend $15,000 to $20,000 a year.

## NINETY-DAY LOVE IT OR LEAVE IT CHALLENGE

mLive offers every doctor our Ninety-Day Love It or Leave It Challenge. With every decision you make in your practice, you are taking a chance. The new treatment coordinator you hire. The new CEREC machine you purchase. Investing in mLive. Of course your imperative is to make a logical decision, not no decision.

Making the logical decision to deploy mLive marketing automation in your practice shouldn't be risky. We know mLive works, and we gladly put our money where our mouth is. When you take our 90-Day Love It or Leave It Challenge, your decision is protected.

Invite our concierge to deploy mLive in your practice. After ninety days you'll see the impressive gains we've made in engaging prospects and patients and creating new opportunities. If you are unsatisfied for any reason, you just say the words, and we refund your monthly membership fees.

## WHAT ARE SOME EXAMPLES?

Let's look at an example of a multistep campaign. A prospect nurturing campaign, for example, is a series of communications designed to capture the attention of the patient over a longer period of time. One of our campaigns expands over forty-nine different days!

Your prospect sees your message on Facebook, which directs to a landing page. She selects that she wants to receive your content. She gives you her name and email address. She downloads and views your engaging content—in this case, a special report—and then answers the prompt to schedule an appointment at your office by selecting her preferred time. All of this without any staff involvement! The campaign follows with a series of multiple emails. Next, we pair it with more social media posts, and if you choose, you can boost it with paid advertising on social media.

Another example is a campaign where you direct prospects to a landing page, they can reserve appointments with you, both on their mobile device and on their desktop, and then they receive appointment confirmation emails as well.

## COMPLETELY CUSTOMIZABLE AND
## TIMELY, CURRENT MESSAGING

Every single campaign in the library can be customized in any way that you want! And every piece of every marketing campaign is personalized to you and your practice with your name, your logo, and all your contact information. If there's something you don't like, you can rewrite anything that you want in the campaign, so you, the doctor, have the ability to customize everything, and it's really, really easy with a timeline interface that shows you all the different steps in the campaign.

## IMPORTANCE OF DATA-DRIVEN BUSINESS DECISIONS

I was taught at an early age by a mentor of mine in business. He said, "Adam, the data will set you free." He followed it up with, "if we're gonna go with opinions, then you know we'll go with mine, but if we're gonna go with the facts and the data, let's go with the facts and the data." The truth is that when we make decisions in our business and our practice on opinions, oftentimes they are wrong, but when we make decisions on facts and data, oftentimes they are right. Business owners, especially doctors, do not have a dashboard that will actually show them the effectiveness of all of the marketing they invest in. With mLive, you have a real-time dashboard that shows every campaign, every person that you assigned to that campaign, how many people clicked, how many people requested appointments, and how much engagement you earned with each person for every campaign.

> *When we make decisions in our business and our practice on opinions, oftentimes they are wrong, but when we make decisions on facts and data, oftentimes they are right.*

## NO DECISION IS A DECISION

Most business owners get a lead, make one phone call, send one email, and if they get no response, they dump the lead in the trashcan and they move to the next person on the list. A patient is not going to come to your chair until, on average, you have connected with him and reached and touched him *five times*. Five times! And unless you create automated systems in your practice to do that for you, you're leaving money on the table. This is exactly what mLive was built to do: *to automate the multistep follow-up, so you can increase the conversion rate of the leads that you're generating.*

You spend money to generate a lead, but until that lead becomes a patient, the money is a complete waste. Most business owners waste 80 percent of their marketing spend because they don't do enough follow-up to convert that lead to a patient. If you're thinking now is not the right time *yet*, then remember the opportunity cost of how many patients you lose each month. How many empty appointments are on your schedule? The cost of not making a decision is greater than the action of getting started with a preloaded, ready-to-go, patient-relationship-building, data and marketing platform.

> *The cost of not making a decision is greater than the action of getting started with a preloaded, ready-to-go, patient-relationship-building, data and marketing platform.*

mLive helps you make *smarter* marketing decisions, to see the exact ROI you get on every dollar you spend. This is revolutionary. We've been working on this for the better part of the year, and we're honored and excited to have the opportunity to grow your practice.

## CHECK TERRITORY AVAILABILITY

mLive is offered to general dentists on a territory exclusive basis. With mLive, you're guaranteed to be one-of-a-kind in your market.

See if your territory is available by visiting **www. mLiveSoftware.com/territory.**

# NOTES

# ABOUT THE AUTHOR

## ADAM WITTY, FOUNDER & CHIEF EXECUTIVE OFFICER

Adam Witty is the Founder and CEO of Advantage, the Business Growth Company. What began in the spare bedroom of his home is now a family of marketing, media, and software businesses that collectively serve thousands of customers in fifty US states and sixty-seven countries.

The Advantage Family includes Advantage Media Group, one of the largest authority marketing companies in the world consisting of the Advantage, Business Journals Books, and ForbesBooks publishing labels; BusinessAdvantage TV, a video-on-demand learning platform for entrepreneurs; Magnetic Marketing, a marketing education company for entrepreneurs; and mLive, new patient marketing automation software for dentists.

Adam was named to the prestigious Inc. 30 Under 30 list of America's Coolest Entrepreneurs in 2011. Advantage has been named to the Inc. 500/5000 list for six of the past eight years. Adam is the author of nine books and has appeared in *USA Today*, *Investor's Business Daily*, *The Wall Street Journal*, and on ABC and FOX. Adam is a leading global expert on "Authority Marketing" and coauthored the best-selling book *Authority Marketing* with Rusty Shelton. Adam's book, *Book the Business: How to Make Big Money with Your Book without Even Selling a Single Copy*, was coauthored with marketing legend Dan Kennedy. Adam's most recent book, *Relentless Implementation*, was coauthored with Alan Mulally, retired CEO of Boeing Commercial Airplanes and Ford Motor Company.

Adam is the Publisher of *Authority Magazine* and *ForbesBooks Review Magazine*. Adam is an Eagle Scout, pilot, member of EO and YPO, and past Board Chair of Clemson University's Spiro Entrepreneurship Institute and nonprofit Youth Entrepreneurship South Carolina. Adam was named Charleston's 2019 Entrepreneur of the Year by the Harbor Entrepreneur Center.

You can learn more about Adam at www. AdamWitty.com or connect with him directly at awitty@advantageww.com.

Printed in the USA
CPSIA information can be obtained
at www.ICGtesting.com
JSHW012044140824
68134JS00033B/3251